Love Changes

A Fresh Start

Minister Octavius Pearson

Bloomington, IN Milton Keynes, UK

authorHOUSE®

AuthorHouse™
1663 Liberty Drive, Suite 200
Bloomington, IN 47403
www.authorhouse.com
Phone: 1-800-839-8640

AuthorHouse™ UK Ltd.
500 Avebury Boulevard
Central Milton Keynes, MK9 2BE
www.authorhouse.co.uk
Phone: 08001974150

First published by AuthorHouse 3/5/2007

ISBN: 978-1-4259-9711-3 (sc)

Library of Congress Control Number: 2007901669

*Printed in the United States of America
Bloomington, Indiana*

This book is printed on acid-free paper.

All Scripture are from the King James Version Bible

Overview

As we go through our lives we have experienced a wide variety of good, as well as our share of bad. We have learned and gained knowledge that we're able to apply in so many areas of our lives.

Just as we have gained this knowledge, so have we shared it. We have found ourselves passing it on to our families, friends, coworkers, and church members. Because of this, we have found ourselves in conversations about the good, the bad and what we have learned. We share the wisdom God has blessed us with from our test and trials.

This reflective study is not designed to answer all of the questions that we have about relationships or marriages. It is designed and purposed to give us a way of thinking that encourages us to explore what we're in. We should look to see if what we have is deeper than anything we have experienced before. Did we settle? Do we have God's blessings all upon our relationships? Is God getting the Glory out of our oneness?

The Bible says that the people parish because of a lack of knowledge. Knowledge used is a tool that will excite our interest and awaken our senses. It compels us to go to that next level that we all are wishing for. This study will give some direction on how we have missed the point of balance and have allowed our goals to be challenged. We will do this through questioning our hopes, our desires and our dreams.

Realize that we can never stop understanding what we have. We must always search for more knowledge. We must grow. We can never become complacent in what we have. We must expect and demand all that God has for us.

So take your time in reading. Allow God to minister to you in your relationships and marriages. Allow Him to open your eyes and your understanding. Listen as He speaks of all the blessings He has for you. Listen as He tells you all that He wants to do for you in your relationships and your marriages.

Love Changes

Table of Contents

Growing As One

Spirit

Of

Relationships

What and how we speak will
Tell all about what we have.

Words Of Wisdom

The word relationship begins with **"re"** which basically means again or back to a previous condition while relationship is having a close connection to a person or thing. Once you **re**connect to your very first love (The spirit established relationship between you and God), you then will be given wisdom and discernment to **re**connect to the person who is purposed for you. When this person is before you, you will feel as if you already have known them. In the physical you are actually **re**-establishing what was previously established in the spirit.

Don't allow life and wrong relationships to beat you up so bad that you lose sight of who you are. Continue to be the beautiful person that you are and when you're **re**connected to your soul mate you won't miss a beat. Your life will be even more enriched. Give to the right one freely and unconditionally and watch it return one hundred fold to you.

From My Wife
Mrs. Michelle Pearson

The Beginning

Relationships, we find ourselves through out our lives involved in so many of them. Do we really know what a relationship is? Do we understand the requirements and the necessity of them? Do we just continue living our lives without them ever becoming complete and meaningful? Do we spend so much time searching and seeking but never finding what it is really about? Do we waste countless days, months and years only to find that it all was for nothing?

Do we stop and look at what we're either in, what we had, or what we are looking for? Do we decide that we cannot live another day, another night or go through another year living this lie? Do we begin working to fix what we have and not stop until we have found that true relationship?

In order to understand what a true relationship is we must learn to learn all over again. We must present ourselves as children seeking to find that one element that has eluded so many of us in our relationships. We must understand what the SPIRIT OF RELATIONSHIP is.

We, for so long, have been misguided about what a relationship is and what it is all about. God is telling us that if we desire and seek after it correctly, that we can find the meaning of a <u>true relationship</u>. He will tell us what it is all about. For to long we have had the wrong focus. We have seen that the people in the Bible have had the wrong focus; as well. We thought it was about the physical or the natural, but this is all a mistake. The main thought by some is always on the physical and it all leads to nothing. God never designed for us to look at the physical first or even the natural because He knows that it is all about the spiritual.

> **Genesis 1:26; 2:7**
> **[26] And God said, Let us make man in our image, after our likeness:**
> **[7] And the LORD God formed man of the dust of the ground, and breathed into his nostrils the breath of life; and man became a living soul.**

Let's look at the first relationship that was established. This was the relationship between God and man. In the book of Genesis God decided to make man. In doing so, God did not just throw Himself out there, but rather He did it perfectly. He made man in His likeness and in His image. Meaning, He made him the way that He wanted man to be. God prepared, designed, and then created man. After all of this, He blew the breath of life into him, establishing a relationship. God showed here that the body was nothing until He blew breath into it.

We have been taught that the relationship came later, but

clearly this is not true. God established the relationship in the spirit. Man has to catch up and then understand what type of relationship he is in. He has to understand the role he has in that relationship. However, it doesn't matter what type of relationship we are in. The relationship is nothing if we do not breathe spiritual life into it.

Just as in God's creation of man there was a purpose, a relationship must also have purpose. A relationship becomes a true relationship when there is a purpose at its foundation. This relationship must be established and not just thrown together. We must learn to be patient in seeking that true relationship. We must allow God to bring that perfect one to us. Begin to search yourself and see why you want to be in a relationship. Search to see why you think you're ready for a relationship. Dig deep to see if you are really ready.

The Focus

There are many different types of relationships. Listed are a few of them that most of us will encounter in our lives.

1. God and man
2. Husband and wife
3. Parents and children
4. Brothers and sisters
5. Boyfriend and girlfriend

At some point in all of these relationships we ask ourselves what has gone wrong. We find ourselves not having that true togetherness we once had. We ask ourselves over and over again, what happened? What happened to the bond we once had, where we could feel that person? What happened to the bond we once had where we could understand that person? What happened that we could no longer sense the hurt and the pain that was going on inside of them? What happened to the bond of caring, sacrifice, suffering and happiness that was once there?

For so long we have beat ourselves up and cried like babies

about what was missing in our relationships. Some people are willing to give it all up and end their lives because of the pain that was going on inside of them. This still does not change what is going on. It doesn't change what is going wrong. It doesn't change the fact that the spirit of unity is missing.

We have been focusing on the negative things of this life and have been missing the true purpose of relationships. We have given up and thrown in the towel of defeat, but God is telling us not to. He will awaken that dormant spirit inside of us. He will show us, once again, the SPIRIT OF RELATIONSHIP.

> *I Samuel 3:1-10*
> *[1] And the child Samuel ministered unto the LORD before Eli. And the word of the LORD was precious in those days; there was no open vision.*
> *[2] And it came to pass at that time, when Eli was laid down in his place, and his eyes began to wax dim, that he could not see;*
> *[3] And ere the lamp of God went out in the temple of the LORD, where the ark of God was, and Samuel was laid down to sleep;*
> *[4] That the LORD called Samuel: and he answered, Here am I.*
> *[5] And he ran unto Eli, and said, Here am I; for thou calledst me. And he said, I called not; lie down again. And he went and lay down.*
> *[6] And the LORD called yet again, Samuel. And Samuel arose and went to Eli, and said, Here am I; for thou didst call me. And he answered, I called not,*

my son; lie down again.
[7] Now Samuel did not yet know the
LORD, neither was the word of the
LORD yet revealed unto him.
[8] And the LORD called Samuel again
the third time. And he arose and went
to Eli, and said, Here am I; for thou
didst call me. And Eli perceived that the
LORD had called the child.
[9] Therefore Eli said unto Samuel, Go,
lie down: and it shall be, if he call thee,
that thou shalt say, Speak, LORD; for
thy servant heareth. So Samuel went
and lay down in his place.
[10] And the LORD came, and stood,
and called as at other times, Samuel,
Samuel. Then Samuel answered, Speak;
for thy servant heareth.

We can also hear the voice of God; however it requires something from us for this to happen. We have to close our eyes and listen as God speaks to us. God is speaking but, for some reason, we have stopped listening to what He is saying. If we're going to go to the next level we must get back to listening to His voice. We see that when God speaks He makes it very clear. Unfortunately, we have closed our minds to Him and can no longer hear Him. Just as God spoke to Samuel in I Samuel the 3rd chapter, He is also speaking to us. The big difference today is that we don't really know how to listen.

Samuel could hear the voice of God even though he did not know it was God. We have become so busy that we are no longer hearing God's voice. Because we don't hear His voice, we're now making mistake after mistake with no end in site. We must do the one thing that was told to Samuel and that is when God speaks, we must speak back.

God has established a spiritual relationship with us. A lot of us don't even know it. God wants to teach, tell, direct and guide us, but we're not listening. In a relationship we must learn to listen and understand what is being said to us. THE SPIRIT OF RELATIONSHIP requires us to listen to what the other person is saying. We can no longer assume what is required; we must know. We can no longer think that things are going to just turn around; we must act. We can no longer wish upon a star that all will be well in the morning; we must do. That is what the SPIRIT OF RELATIONSHIP is all about. It is about being productive in the spirit and not just in the physical. It was never designed for the spirit to enhance the physical, but for the physical to enhance the spiritual. Once we get a grasp on this our relationships will be elevated to the level that it is suppose to be.

> **St. John 10:10**
> **[10] The thief cometh not, but for to steal, and to kill, and to destroy: I am come that they might have life, and that they might have it more abundantly.**

God is telling us not to lose focus on what He ordained relationships to be. We must not allow the devil to corrupt our lives leaving us empty. We must learn to fight for that which is ours. God has told us day in and day out that it is our life and we have a choice in it. We must take it back if we really want it. We can have that happy home where true love is everyday. We can have peace in the mist of the storm but it is all about what we make of it. The SPIRIT OF RELATIONSHIP can only happen when we desire it to happen. Although God gives, it is up to us to activate. God shows, but it is up to us to trigger His power. It is God who allows, but it is up to us to have the will to make it all happen. Believe it or not it all starts with having a positive and focused mind.

The Responsibility

Some of us believe we are the way we are because of a family curse. Some say that our up bringing, or the lack there of, is the cause for our lives being the way they are. Just like anything else, we refuse to take ownership of what is going on in our lives.

Some say that it is the white man that did this. Some say it is this black man or the foreigners that has brought the mess into our lives. For most of us, we will never say it was or it is us. We never take ownership of the things that have come into our lives. We never admit that we have destroyed our own relationships. We never admit that we have allowed mess and negative stuff to penetrate that once happy home. Finally, we feel our relationship is not even worth going home to or fighting for anymore.

We must ask ourselves, what happened? We once had a happy home but it is all gone. We had a wonderful husband or wife. We had very loving children. We can never seem to put our fingers on it, but it is staring us right in the face, "responsibility". We're responsible for the happiness that is going on in our lives. It is not the husband's job nor is it the wives', or even the children's, but it is our own responsibility. Everyone else simply adds to what we bring to ourselves.

We place blame on everyone except ourselves. If we take the time to examine ourselves we will see that we could have done something different that would have made the difference. We should have read the hand writings on the wall. If we had done this, then we would not be kicking ourselves about what is going on, what we're going through or what we have lost.

> **2 Peter 2:9**
> **[9] The Lord knoweth how to deliver the godly out of temptations, and to reserve the unjust unto the day of judgment to be punished:**

When we step outside of God we must learn to accept our punishment. We think that God is going to do something to fix it all, but that may not be the case. In accepting responsibility, we must understand that we have a choice. We choose who we deal with. We choose who we allow into our lives. We must understand the consequences for allowing the negative people to come into our world. There are always red flags that we choose to ignore. **So yes, we do in fact know**.

God has given us everything we need to have a happy and productive life. God only requires us to follow His directions. We cannot live our lives so free hearted and think that all will be well. We cannot think one sided. We cannot expect people to conform to our ways or vise versa. Just as we cannot teach old dog new tricks or give a zebra its stripes, the same applies to us and everyone else. We must accept that person which God has given us and learn to grow with him\her.

This does not apply if that person is not what you need and was not given to you by God. It's another thing when that person was never designed for you. It's something else when that person you're with cannot take you to the next level of life in the spirit. These are just a few things that we must search ourselves and take full responsibility for. It is our mistake that our lives are so empty. We must take it personal so when God does fix it, the same mistakes will never happen again.

God gives us another chance to make it right. He sometimes does it by taking us out of that relationship. He may give us that zeal back to love the mate we're with, or give us someone else. We must ask ourselves are we really ready for the challenges that are going to come to us? Are we ready to be true to ourselves and to the other person? Are we going to do the same thing we did in our past resulting in another wasted life? We must remember that our decision does not just matter to us but it also matters to everyone else in our lives, (from our mates, to our friends, to our children and most of all to ourselves). It affects everyone.

The Difference

What is the problem? Why can we not find and maintain that wonderful and bliss relationship? Why do they almost always have to end? Where has that bonded, secured, honest, faithful, pure and true relationship gone? These are questions that we all are asking. We can find people talking about it in church, on the job, in the beauty salons, barber shops, on the bus, internet, TV, radio and even in our homes. Why is it a universal conversation? Why is it a talk that has gone on for ages?

This timeless conversation is a major issue in all of our lives. Because we do not have that true relationship, we're now in dysfunctional relationships. We have to deal with mess in so many different ways. We see how damaging these relationships are. We see how it is destroying, mentally as well as physically, and is corrupting the very foundation of that which is supposes to have been true. We have seen its destruction as young teenagers (when we first started noticing the opposite sex) and have had to deal with it all of our adult lives. For some reason we have not found that one relationship that has it all. We have found ourselves in relationships that are missing and lacking the very fiber of the foundation that we need.

We must ask ourselves why we cannot have that TV relationship. Why do we think our lives are fairy tales when things are going right? Why do we think our lives are normal when things are going wrong? We think our lives are standard when our lives are out of control. Why do we accept mess and issues that come into our lives and say that it is all we can get? Why do we think we should be content with mess? Why do we think we don't deserve better? How did we allow ourselves to become comfortable in misery?

We're not really looking at our relationships the way that we're suppose to be looking at them. Just as our relationship is to be with God, we must realize it is the same for the person that is in our lives. Both relationships are suppose to last forever.

What we must learn to realize is that there is suppose to be a difference in relationships. It is not business as usual when it comes to something that is true and pure. It is about having that divine purpose. That's what we're in. We must allow God to perfect it in us. The difference in a true relationship is the fact that the spiritual aspect is the most important part of it.

The Other Spirit

We find ourselves looking at our relationships that we are in or once were in, and begin to ask ourselves, **what changed**? We do not know what formed that relationship into something crazy. What caused it to be out of control? When did it become dysfunctional? How did we allow it to become damaging mentally, as well as physically? Why is it now unhealthy to everyone that is involved?

We look back over our experiences and cannot understand what may have caused all of this. It is not the finance, but it has its place. It is not the sex, but it has its place. It is not the fact of the way they kept the home. It isn't even the fact they stayed at home, but they too had their place of causing problems. ___It's about allowing the wrong spirit to come into it___.

> **Deuteronomy 11:16**
> **[16] Take heed to yourselves, that your heart be not deceived, and ye turn aside, and serve other gods, and worship them;**

We must begin to look at what type of spirit we have allowed into our relationships. As we begin to slow down and look at our relationships, God will show us what spirit is actually there. We can see if we have the spirit of bondage. Some men and women have this spirit and try to control the other person. There may be the spirit of covertness where we try to get what the Jones' has at any cost. We may even have the spirit of simply flesh where we just try, in all aspects, to get over either through lying, cheating, being irresponsible, uncaring or being selfish.

We have become selfish to our own desires and have lost what relationships are really all about. This may be the case because we're dealing with it from a life aspect rather than from a spiritual aspect. Most of us do not know why or how we have allowed the wrong spirit into our lives. We don't know how to get it out and get things back to the way they are suppose to be. We must get it together. We cannot survive any other way. We cannot survive thinking everything will just work no matter what. That is a lie. We're lying to ourselves because the wrong spirit will always tell us that it will workout, **until it is too late**.

When we learn to focus and understand what spirit we're dealing with, we must either grow with it if it is right or let it go if it is wrong. The wrong spirit has destroyed homes, families and relationships. It has caused men, as well as women, to do illogical and irrational things. When we look back, we cannot come up with an honest reason behind it.

We have talked to and have known people that have

done wrong to other people's properties, harmed them physically or harmed themselves because of it. Negative things happen to us when we allow that negative spirit to dictate our lives and relationships.

There is a solution to all of this. It requires total surrender and transformation from where we are and what we're about. We must begin to believe in what our relationships should be. God has designed relationships to be special and meaningful and even more importantly, to last forever. We must understand that negative spirits will destroy the way of life that God has for His people. They will leave everything dead and destroyed.

It is not too late to get that other spirit out of our homes and out of our relationships. It will take something that we all do not want to do. It will take us starting over. We must make that decision today; for tomorrow is never promised to us. We think that we have more time, but we have had far too many times and now it is too late. We moved too late, reacted too late, understood too late, realized too late and began to care too late. At this point, reality sets in. This is also when we began to understand that it is all over and gone.

The wrong spirit destroys and tears down. It corrupts our minds. It places thoughts of confusion that were never there. It makes us think bad thoughts of things that would never happen. It makes us fantasize about other people and other things keeping us from seeing what we really have. As long as we have an ounce of love we can stop this spirit from anymore damaging influences.

Thoughts On Relationships

My Mom – Mrs. Catherine Pearson
Keep your faith and trust in Jesus. Keep on going.
   Keep the family first in your life after God.

My Wife – Mrs. Michelle Pearson
To find love is a treasure. To recognize love is a gift.
   To experience love is a blessing. To intertwine
   your lives because of love is truly divine.

Couple of 40 years
As a couple you never stop dating. You never stop
   doing that which you did to get and find that
   person.

Pastor Marion Solomon – Mt. Zion Apostolic Church
Hebrews 13:4a – Marriage is honorable in all. God
   has ordained marriage from the beginning of
   time. Marriage is the visible union in the earth
   realm that mirrors the union in the spirit realm
   of Christ and His bride the church. To have
   success in marriage operate Godly principles that
   guarantees Godly results.

Pastor Robert Williams – New Dawn Baptist Church
The real love and strength in a marriage comes from within. From a close loving contact of your spirit with God's spirit makes your life together conformed to what God wants it to be. Always remember that you can always depend on God to make it what it should always be.

Pastor Kelvin McNeil – The Body of Christ Church
Keep Christ at the center of the marriage. Focus on building a strong friendship. Healthy communication is essential.

Sister Rena McNeil – The Body of Christ Church
Couples that pray together ultimately stay together. Don't forget the family prayers.

Final Thoughts

When we stop what we're doing, wake up, and realize how our relationships really are, (that their much different from how it is supposed to be) then and only then will we learn to search out for change. We cannot allow our lives and our families to be destroyed from a lack of understanding. God is telling us and is giving us another chance to fix it all. We have seen too much misery, too many fights and too many hearts broken because we fail to make things right with choices we make.

There is a resolution for all of this negativity we have too often seen. Our minds, for some, do not believe a corrective action is possible. Believe what you feel deep inside. When God is at the center, you will allow positive things to be the foundation. You will constantly be looking for God in everything. At this point you will then take life and your relationship more seriously.

It is also about having that person in your life that is going in the same direction as you are. We can never get to where we're trying to go as long as we're fighting each other and not working together. Relationships are work, and never forget it. Who is to say that you cannot enjoy the work that you're doing. Begin to enjoy your job and see your job start to enjoy you.

Finally, we must look at this society that we're in. We must begin to see that the way this world does everything goes not only against God, but against the true way that a relationship is supposed to be. Take a look at how this world deals with every situation. Take notice that it is all about a negative and irresponsible way of life. However, it is all not over. Begin to focus, take responsibility and understand what a relationship is all about. Begin to look at how that relationship started. Begin to do exactly that once again. Also when looking at the world do the complete opposite of what it tells you to do. Begin to look more to God to see Him truly open your eyes to the things that He has for you. Then watch happiness, joy and peace come back into that relationship that you're in.

Your relationship is all about what you put in and you're the one that will make or break it. When I say **"you"**, I mean the two people that are in it. It is not a one sided affair, but rather a collective affair. It takes two to make it right or make it wrong. Begin to speak life into that relationship and believe that God put you together. Your relationship is not a mistake or unrecoverable, but it will only be what you make it. Believe in what you both have and begin to take it back to the beginning. Work like you've never worked before to make your relationship what you both have always desired it to be.

Find trust, find honesty, find love, find happiness and most of all find God and see just how different it will be. When the SPIRIT OF RELATIONSHIP is your foundation, it will be like nothing else on earth. So remember, then and only then, will your relationship be heaven sent.

Spirit Of Relationships Notes

_____
_____
_____
_____
_____
_____
_____
_____
_____
_____
_____
_____
_____
_____
_____
_____
_____
_____
_____
_____
_____
_____
_____
_____
_____
_____
_____
_____

Love

Unmeasured

The power that we have to control
Our present and direct our
Future is based on how we deal with our past

Searching Wrong

People look at us and see so much, but in our own minds what do we really see? Who are we really seeing and are we happy with what we're looking at? We have searched for an answer from so many sources, but we have failed to ask the right source. We therefore, miss the whole meaning of what we have been looking for. We ask the question, why are we not happy? Why are we in so much misery? Why can't we come out of it and find happiness?

It seems as if we have searched endlessly from one end of the earth to the other, but cannot find love. We have put in so much time and effort, but still cannot find true love. We have emptied our bank accounts thinking that we can buy love, but to no avail, there is still nothing. We find ourselves having to start all over, searching again.
The answer does not lie in what we're doing, but in what we're not doing. We're going about it with good intentions, but doing it with the wrong tools. We think that if we're able to talk, walk, think and act the part, then all will be well. This is a myth. At the end of the

day we still find ourselves in the same situation as we started. We are left alone and empty inside.

We fail to realize when we're searching, that we must understand the method of searching. The Bible speaks on the matter of when a man finds a wife he finds a good thing. A man that finds his true love finds someone that has favor with God. God honors marriages, but He can only honor them when it is done in obedience to His word. We must find out how God wants us to search after our mate and where to find out mate. It is then and only then that we can find true happiness and be able to live the life that God has designed for us.

> *Proverbs 18:20-22*
> *[20] A man's belly shall be satisfied with the fruit of his mouth; and with the increase of his lips shall he be filled. [21] Death and life are in the power of the tongue: and they that love it shall eat the fruit thereof. [22] Whoso findeth a wife findeth a good thing, and obtaineth favour of the LORD.*

The Bible says that the man is to speak about what he has and to keep it on his lips, for then he shall be filled. It is first about what we speak into our lives. If we speak life into finding that mate, then God will bring that mate to us. If we speak any other thing we will miss the full increase of what God has for us.

We must understand that it is all about what we allow to penetrate the very fiber of our lives. We can no longer allow ourselves to become weary in our search. We have jumped in and out of relationships. We seem to never get to the point within our spirits, minds or hearts that God has someone special for us. There is a special person waiting for all of us.

There is a right way to find love. We have to become more aware of what the right way is. We have to look at finding our mates more seriously than we have ever before. We have found love avoiding us. We have found mess trapping us. We cannot seem to stop this endless madness. **NEWS FLASH** - we cannot give up! If God has created that one, then we must believe, trust and never give up until we find them.

Settling For Little

It is amazing how we can look back over our lives and see the mistakes that we have made. We talk about it in our conversations. We say if we knew then what we know now, we would not have done what we did. It is good to look back if we're able to grow from it. Some of us can't handle looking back. It is a mistake. We continuously look back accepting that which is not for us. We settle for so little.

Looking back can be a terrible thing when our past is controlling our future. It dictates our happiness, creates barriers, and forms walls of separation causing loneliness and emptiness. We must understand that our past is just like the Bible. It is a tool used to take us higher and further in our lives. God is our schoolmaster teaching us that we do not have to settle for less. We don't have to settle for less in our relationship with Him or anyone else. We must learn to challenge who we are. What we demand from our today, based on what we have learned from our past, dictates our future.

We must look at where we are trying to go in our lives and compare it to where we already have been. Try to see the total picture. If it is a job, then look at it. If it is a person, then look at them, if it is a home, become aware of it. Also, we need to look at ourselves and wake up to reality. We must truly see what we are worth. We must not settle for anything less than what God has promised us. We have gotten into bad situations, made bad decisions, and listened to those stupid voices. Why? We need to wake up and realize that we have settled. Now we are kicking ourselves. We are angry at ourselves because in our spirits we knew that we deserved more. We knew we were better than that.

We have lost so much by settling. We see this settling spirit going on all too often and in too many instances. What is even worse is that this way of thinking has not just infected us, but also our children. We're no longer looking for what is right, but what is comfortable. Instead of what is best, we are willing to settle for what we have which is nothing. This mindset has messed us and our children up very badly. We can't even help them because we're stuck in the same rut. We act as if we're unable to help ourselves, as well as them.

We find this settling spirit so often that we have said it controls and affects us in almost everything we do. When we settle, we not only put ourselves in bondage, but we also shackle the blessings of God. When He does send His blessings, we're unable to recognize His blessings as something good and beneficial to us. God is looking to open our eyes to this settling spirit that has made its way into our comfortable homes. He wants us to see just how much more we can have. He wants us to see just how happy our lives could truly be.

Deuteronomy 23:5
[5] ....but the LORD thy God turned the curse into a blessing unto thee, because the LORD thy God loved thee

God is telling us that we do not have to worry about our past. He is going to turn what we thought was a curse into a blessing. God is telling us that His people are not cursed even when it seems like they are. Since we're not cursed, we do not have to settle for anything less then what He has for us. God's desire is to bring happiness to us. He wants to show that He is God and that no matter what has gone on in our lives He is still in control.

Deserving More

We have to look at ourselves and begin to speak life. We must speak growth into our future. For so long, we have spoken death, struggles, pain, poverty and every other kind of negative thing. Understand that our words and proclamations over our lives have more affect on our future than we think. We must ask ourselves how much do we really deserve? Do we deserve all the struggles that we have put ourselves through? Do we deserve every blessing, all the happiness and all the joy that God has for us?

We say to ourselves that we have so much to offer, but what about how much they have to offer us. **Love Unmeasured** is all about what we desire and all we deserve. We cannot compromise who we are just to say that we have something or someone. We must look at ourselves as if we deserve more. We deserve the best. We must look at our past and see how we have settled, then take that knowledge and start focusing on what we deserve.

St. Matthew 7:7
Ask, and it shall be given you; seek, and ye shall find; knock, and it shall be opened unto you:

We must understand that we must learn to ask God for what we want. It is not that He is just going to give it all to us, we need to ask for wisdom. We must learn to search ourselves and get an understanding of what is needed in our lives, as well. God is a God that is looking for us to come to Him and ask for what we want. He says for us to ask and it shall be given. He knows what it is that we need, but He wants us to understand it as well. It is one thing for a parent to know it is time to feed his/her kids, but it is another thing when that child knows that it is time to eat. God is waiting for us to come to that understanding that it is our time to be happy and complete with all the blessings He has waiting for us. We must understand that asking is a form of speaking. We must speak it into existence. We must ask in faith. He will deliver. God will answer our prayers.

Our tongue holds life and death. Our tongue holds success and failure. It's about what we speak in our lives. The things we want won't be in our lives until we make those things a priority and speak positively about those things. It should be apparent that how we speak to our situation normally will come to past. We must learn how to speak specifically on that which we really want. There is another thing besides the tongue that dictates our future and that other thing is called DEMAND.

We must demand happiness in our lives. We must demand peace, unity, joy and most of all, love. It all starts within us first. This is not just a word coming out of our mouths, but an action and a reaction to life. Love is a two way street. It requires two people to make it happen. Love is not an overnight sensation, but a spirit that overtakes and will change our lives forever. What is missing is the demand, the will, the desire and the challenge to make it all what we want.

One problem with trying to bring positive things into a relationship is that we sometimes attribute it to being weak. We think it causes us to be soft. Even though the positive thing may be of good intentions, it still can be viewed in a weak manner. When we put a demand on things like love, respect, honesty and caring, then and only then will it be viewed as strength. Increase your standards. Some people may take it in the wrong way. They may even show it in the wrong way, but, in both cases, it is still about one being strong. What does demand do? It places responsibility upon that relationship. It challenges the structure of that relationship and most of all, it places order in that relationship. Of course all of these things can only come out when the demand has that positive base. It must have that center core which is God.

Everyone tells us when we come out of a relationship that it takes time to get over that person and to find ourselves. Why do they tell us this? What is it that we must get over? Why do we need to find ourselves? The person that is going through or coming out of a bad relationship can only answer these questions. We must have that time to look back and reflect on the things that are now in our past. Then we need to open our eyes and begin to see where we really are today. After the dust clears, we can now see what demands are really needed in our lives to bring us to that point of true love. We can see that we don't need to settle for anything. We can see the need to increase our standards. We need to expect more and demand more.

Starting Over

We now know that we deserve more in our lives. We cannot settle for less than what God has for us. For most of our lives we have been neglected and unappreciated, but now there is something different in our lives. That new thing is something that God continues to give us and that is another chance. God gives us another day for us to get things right not just with Him, but also with ourselves. Everyday that we can wake up and see the beauty of this world, He is telling us that we have a new day. In that new day, it is all about what we have prayed and cried all night for. We have missed it, wished for it, and desired it. It is a fresh start, a new beginning or simply another chance.

Now it is your day to receive the blessings that are found in **Love Unmeasured**. It is your day to come into true and uncompromising compassion that you have never felt before. Because you have not given up and thrown in the towel of defeat, it is your season. Everyday you will wake up more determined than the day before. This is what God looks for in us. He wants us to realize we can conquer the curse. We can become free from our strongholds. We deserve **Love Unmeasured**, unlimited, and uninhibited.

> *Jeremiah 18:1-7*
> *[1] The word which came to Jeremiah from the LORD, saying,*
> *[2] Arise, and go down to the potter's house, and there I will cause thee to hear my words.[3] Then I went down to the potter's house, and, behold, he wrought a work on the wheels.*
> *[4] And the vessel that he made of clay was marred in the hand of the potter: so he made it again another vessel, as seemed good to the potter to make it.*
> *[5] Then the word of the LORD came to me, saying,*
> *[6] O house of Israel, cannot I do with you as this potter? saith the LORD. Behold, as the clay is in the potter's hand, so are ye in mine hand, O house of Israel.*

God is molding and making us everyday of our lives. He is doing this so we can become complete in Him. Just as God is molding us, He is also molding our mates that we may also be complete. It is a beautiful thing to find that one that can truly love you and you truly love them back. Many of us have never seen this type of love in our relationships. God has given us another chance. He lets us know we're always in His hands. Our lives are like step ladders. We can always go up to that next level. So take the next level up. Everything that God allows in our lives is used to bring us closer and closer to that happiness that we deserve.

The one thing that is so great about God giving us another chance, is the fact that we find out that true love is worth all that we had gone through. We now have enough strength that nothing ever again is going to stop us from reaching our goals. Now we can tell the world that it was God that did it. It was God that made us go right instead of going left. It was God that brought us to that location where our soul mate was waiting for us. Through all this, we know that it will always be God that will keep us focused. Nothing will stop or deter us from keeping what we have found.

My Love My Friend

St. John 15:12-13
[12] This is my commandment, That ye
love one another, as I have loved you.
[13] Greater love hath no man than
this, that a man lay down his life for his
friends.

God has given us many commandments, but one in particular takes us to a higher love with the person that we're with. He commanded us to love with not just any kind of love, but a love which supersedes any other. Ok, we know that we are required to love everyone. But just as God has that special love for His people, so are we to have that special love with that special one.

God expresses the level of love that is unmeasured and unsurpassed with more than mere words. We have the Bible as a tool, guidance and life operating manual. His words are life, truth and love. We also experience mercy and grace daily in which His love extends to infinity. Love is increased constantly and grows with every waking moment.

The Bible talks about no greater love than a person that can lay down his life for a friend. First, of all that special one is your friend and not just any kind of a friend. Are the ones that we call friends truly of the status to be called a friend? We must first find out what is a friend.

The Webster dictionary says a friend is a person on intimate and affectionate terms with another. Intimate means one that is close in personal relations; familiar; closely allied. So, what is this person in normal terms? A friend is one that is connected to the point that they know all about us and we know all about them. We are allies or joined together to help each other. We are there for that person and they're there for us in the good days, as well as the bad. A friend will go the extra mile. A friend will give their all to reach the goals that are set before them.

What is that heavenly sent friend supposed to possess that none other has? What is inside of them that can reach so deep in us that mere minds can never understand? What is so different in them that can touch so deep and reach so high in us? What that person possesses is the truthfulness of oneness and togetherness. They also possess friendship to the next level. It is not just what they possess for us, but also, what we possess for them; **our heaven sent friend**.

God is showing here the level of love that is not present in some relationships. We don't care, not even a little bit, and we surely do not reach the level that we're willing to give all. Yes, that is what God is talking about. Giving all for that one that we love, willing to sacrifice all, even our lives, for that special one. We also knowing that the one we love will do the same for us. This is what God desires for that relationship that He has designed and has put together. This can only be achieved when the one we're with is connected to us from the hip and from the heart.

We cannot take our relationships lightly. We must look at them deeper than we have ever before. The reason being, they are deeper than anything that we have ever experienced before. The only thing that is greater in experience is that of our relationship with God. Even our relationships with our children cannot reach this level. It is connected in the spirit, the natural, the heart, the mind and in every fiber of our being.

This is a tremendous level that we're talking about. Our love for our children is always and will always remain unbreakable, but there is another love. This other love is set for that one that is not blood, but is just as great, if not greater. This love is for those soul mates that God has designed for us. We are one in the same with them.

Final Thoughts

We must ask ourselves some questions. Are the mates that we have truly our friends? Are these people the one that is there for us? Are they our Heavenly sent friends? God's purpose in our lives is clearly defined. There should be a clearly defined purpose for our mate, as well. Love is a special thing. It is a beautiful experience and one that we must have in this life. We must first understand that it is a give and take situation that LOVE incorporates.

Just as our relationship with God demands more, we must demand so much more from our earthly relationships. We must demand that our relationships be first in our lives, only behind our relationship with God. We cannot just think that it is just something to experience. We must understand that it is a lifestyle. We must require, demand and expect to give to it and receive from it everyday of our lives. We must also look at ourselves and believe that we deserve the best out of it.

Anyone can go to the movies with us. Anyone can go with us to dinner. Anyone can have sex with us, but there is only one that we can give true love to. That special one is the mate that God has designed and has given us. Don't settle for a mere hot dog when you can have steak. Your relationship should be a buffet of happiness. Don't settle for less than you deserve. Look at yourself and see that you deserve more, expect more, and require more. Guess what, and then you will have more. A lot of times the negative experiences that go on in relationships are because we have allowed them. Don't get me wrong, some of it is God and some is the devil, but a lot of it is us.

God has placed us so high and even He acknowledges us as great people. We are supposed to look at ourselves in the same light. Just as we give greatness, we should expect greatness. It is not that we're so high and mighty about who we are, but it is about what we have to offer and what they have to offer to us in return. We settle for less than the greatness that God has for us.

So remember **Love Unmeasured** is something that God measures. This measurement is the fact that, that person is the one for us. We have to be willing to give all, receive all, and go to that level above and beyond. God can now bless, because we're connected, we're joined and we're one with the mate that He has given us.

> *Remember, just as your love for God and His unmeasured love for you cannot be measured, so is your love for the one He has sent.*

Love Unmeasured Notes

_____
_____
_____
_____
_____
_____
_____
_____
_____
_____
_____
_____
_____
_____
_____
_____
_____
_____
_____
_____
_____
_____
_____
_____
_____
_____
_____
_____
_____

Left

In The

Past

The power that we have to control
Our present and direct our
Future is based off how we deal with our past

It's Not Dead

We look at our past and what we have been through knowing that we have so many questions that need answers. What's bad is the fact that we do not have the answers. We look at where we are and say that we have lost so much. We ask ourselves what is our lives really worth? What are our lives about? We have thought and pondered because God has not moved in the timely fashion (to meet our needs) we desired. Now we think it is all a waste and that nothing positive will ever come to us or from us.

We cannot look at our past in this manner. This is just what the devil wants us to do. He does not want us to see who we are or what we have in God. He wants us to look at what we don't have and focus on all the mess and negative things that have gone on in our lives. Even though we have focused our minds, we must understand that our lives are really worth something. We just need to find out what and how much. We must understand and remember that God has more waiting for us.

We look around and we see so much pain. We see so much misery. We go through our days wondering and wishing but so many of our days end worse than they began. We ask ourselves how much more can we take? How much longer do we really have to remain in this dysfunctional, unbearable and displeasing relationship? How long do we remain in those lonely places where the only noise is the weeping of emptiness? What about the crying of sorrow that is coming from our hearts? These emotions are strongly expressed through the tears that are flowing down our faces.

But God expresses to us His love in our everyday lives. He lets us know that what ever we're in is never dead. Even though others may say it is, until God says it is, then it is not. We all have in our lives one thing although we use very little of it. It is called **time**. We do not give adequate time to anything any more and we definitely do not give the effort needed to see if it is alive or dead. We're willing to just throw it all away and end it all. In doing this, we must remember that we're not just giving up on that relationship, but we're giving up a ton of time, a ton of effort, a mountain of finances and a life time of emotions and feelings. We must look at the signs and wonders that God blesses to be around us. We can see this especially in the field of farming and planting. Just as a farmer tills the ground to wake up the enriched soil for his crops to grow properly, the same is for us in our relationships. We must shake ourselves, quicken the spirit inside of us, and begin to work on our relationships. Work on them until fruit is produced and they return back to what they once were from the beginning. Work on them until they have the richness and fertility they once had.

All God needs is a little life to grow a forest and that is the same for us. All we need is a little love, a little compassion, a little caring, a little belief and a little trust to turn those relationships around and bring them back to life. Bring those relationships back to what can once again be cherished and loved.

> *Proverbs 3:5-6*
> *[5]Trust in the LORD with all thine heart; and lean not unto thine own understanding.*
> *[6]In all thy ways acknowledge him, and he shall direct thy paths*

God wants us to trust in Him. In trusting, we must believe in Him and follow Him for He knows the way back to what we have lost. We know that our relationship will never be anything unless God fixes it. God can never do this unless we leave our problems, our issues and our troubles in the past. We cannot hold on to the mistakes that we have made or even the ones that our mates have made. For as God forgives, so should we.

Everyday we live we have the potential to fall, to make a mistake, to sin or to do wrong in this life. There is one thing that we must keep in front of our minds; that God always is present. In God there is grace and in His grace there is forgiveness. Just as God shows grace to us and forgets about the mistakes that we have made, so should we forgive and leave what we were delivered from in the past.

God's love grows and is shown more when we fall. He increases His presence in our lives when we turn from Him. He speaks even more to us when we're going in the wrong direction and doing wrong in our lives. The one thing that we must learn to do more of is learn to listen to God and see what He is telling us to do. We don't listen and hear what God is telling us. God is trying to take us ahead so we must leave the past behind.   In order to do this we must do the opposite of what the flesh tells us. If our mind tells us to stop, then we must go further. If it tells us to turn, then keep going straight and if it tells us to leave, then stay. In all these things there must be the presence of God which will ensure that all will get turned around and will get fixed by Him.

God is looking and waiting to take us higher. In order for this to take place, both people must stop looking back and go forward expecting change. Expect that which was missing to come back, and once again be all that it was and more. God can bring it back but it takes both people to believe.   He can make it live once again. This can never happen with only one person. It requires both truly believing and acting upon what they believe.

When we have faith that God can do the impossible, we can look into our lives just a little bit deeper and believe just a little bit stronger than we did before. But if we have given up already then God, in most cases, has nothing to work with. God never gave up on the woman with the issue of blood. God never gave up on the lame man at the pool. God never gave up on the man that was possessed by the demons. He did not give up on the boy that was dead. This is the same for us in our lives today. He has not given up on us. We have demons, we have issues, and we have brokenness in relationships that makes us think we're dead. Just like in the woman, the boy and the men, God came in and fixed them all. God wants to come into our situations and do the same for us. He wants to deliver, mend, fix, and restore. He wants to bring us out. He also wants to give back to us what we have lost. So keep believing in God and watch Him do what He wants to do. Watch Him do what He said He will do.

God wants to repair our relationships that we're already in. He wants to mend those marriages that seem to be damaged beyond repair and revitalize those relationships that seem to be dead. God is still speaking to us and telling us that it is not dead. He will bring live to those relationships and marriages once again.

Time To Move On

For some relationships and marriages that we have not allowed God to fix, they are **now dead**. There is no life, no feeling, and no love. We must come to the revelation that it is over. It is time to move on. We now need to find a way to bounce back from our past, break that mindset of failure and begin to start over.

We have to open our eyes because we have been blinded to the problems and issues that had gone wrong in our past. We either did not understand it, or even worse, did not want to recognize what had gone wrong in it. For some odd reason we want to hold on to the past even though God has given us the means to start over. He also has given us the means to leave our past in the past. God tells us to go on to perfection or to go to the next level in life. It is amazing how many of us do not do this. We hold on to negativity, we hold on to the things that have hurt us and we especially hold on to those things that have kept us down. We clinch to those things that have kept us from gaining and receiving that which God wants to give us.

There is so much more waiting for us and we do not even know it. God has opened doors and has delivered so many blessings to us. Unfortunately, we have closed our minds and our hearts to the fact that God has given us the ability to move on. He has given us the ability to receive what He has for us, **today**. Moving on is not jumping into something else, but getting out, finding yourself, and understanding where you are. It is not excepting the mess from the past or getting into new mess. It is about finding the balance within oneself. It is allowing God to mend the broken heart, fill the emptiness of loneliness, and kill the misery. God is telling us not to stop seeking after Him, but open ourselves to new blessings that are for us.

There is a statement that we have heard but have ignored for so long, and that is "leave the past in the past". We can never allow ourselves to do this and be able to move on. We must learn to listen to the voice of God and seek healing. This healing is essential for us to make it to tomorrow. So many people can never get a good night sleep or simply rest in order to make it to tomorrow. Moving on is not just necessary for you, but for everyone that is in your life. It is also for everything that you deal with. If you cannot move on, it will affect your job, your home, your friends and especially your life as a whole.

We talk about this healing that we need, but why do we not talk about or deal with the issue of moving on? Why is moving on such a negative thing? Why can we not realize that, in a lot of cases, it is necessary? Why can we not let go? Why can we not leave alone the negative and move on to what we know will make our lives so much better? It is because we're dealing with things all wrong. We're dealing with everything that has happened to us today as if we can change what had happened in our past. If the life that we once had is over and what we once had is dead, then we must leave it alone because we cannot revitalize things that are completely dead. One of the major things that most councilors tell people is to open up to the truth that is before them. The truth for some is the fact that old relationships are over. If God blesses you again to get into another one, then leave that old one and all of its baggage in the past.

It is a great lesson to learn from your past. That is what we all should do. Look and see what you did that made that person happy and use it. Look at what made that person love you and use it. Look at what made that person appreciate you and apply it. Be careful not to make the mistake of thinking that new person is the same as the old one. Modify what you have learned, change it to fit what you have now, and move on up to a higher level of love that you have found. God allows us to go through for a reason. God punishes us for a reason and God blesses us for a reason. The problem is not God, but it is us. We don't use what we have learned to make us better, but we use what we have learned to mess up what we have currently. This occurs because we have not moved on. We have not learned to "Let Go and Let God."

Frustrated

It is amazing that even when we have gone through and have dealt with so much that we still cannot break out of where we are and get past what we're in. We have been in abusive (mentally or physically) relationships and we know that we need to move on, but still can't. Why is it so hard to let it go or leave the mess in the past? The good news is not the fact that we can't, because we can. We just don't make the choice to move past it. The reason being, we have not gotten frustrated enough to get over it. We have not gotten tired of being beat down and whipped on, over and over again. When we get to this point, then we can leave it all in the past.

It is not just when we are in abusive relationships, (these are just the extreme ones), but in all relationships that are bad, we must get tired of being in something that we know is not going anywhere. Staying can be a very big mistake. We should not want to go back to a dead situation and try to find something alive in it when we know that there is nothing there.

> ### St. Luke 15:16-18
> *[16] And he would fain have filled his belly with the husks that the swine did eat: and no man gave unto him.*
>
> *[17] And when he came to himself, he said, How many hired servants of my father's have bread enough and to spare, and I perish with hunger!*
>
> *[18] I will arise and go to my father, and will say unto him, Father, I have sinned against heaven, and before thee,*

We must get to the point of understanding that by allowing ourselves to return back to a dead situation we belittle ourselves. We not only shame ourselves, but we're also being a shame to God Himself. God has told us over and over again who we are. We have allowed our situations, people and things to tell us differently. We have become so blind to who we are that we will allow just about anything and anyone into our world. We must look at ourselves, see that we are, and do just as this son did. Come to your self, start seeing who you are and see where you are.

Not only did he come to himself and see where he was, but he got frustrated about where he was. We must get this way about the things that are going wrong or have gone wrong in our lives. It is our time now to take it all back. Just see what he did and see if you have enough strength inside of you to do the same. First, he almost made the mistake of eating with the swine which is the lowest point any human being could ever go. He saw what he was about to do. Second, he looked at himself.

Third, he looked at who he was. Fourth, he got up. These are some of the things that we must learn to do when we become frustrated about where we are. We must look at what we're doing, where we are, and who we are. We must look at how we are living and take control of it. Find an answer to fixing it all.

Apparently, for some strange reason, we can never get frustrated enough to see where we are. We walk around in a fog. God is ready to clear it all up. God's desire is to open our eyes to all the problems, all the mess and all the issues that we're in. He is looking to bring us out. In all this, God is also looking for us to get to the point in our lives that we take a stand on who we are. We need to find a way of getting back to where we know we're supposed to be. God never designed for His people to be stuck in mess or remain in the situations that we have allowed ourselves to get into. He designed these situations for us to learn and grow. So the question we must ask ourselves is how frustrated are we? What are we going to do to change where we are?

To get to our change we are required to become focused. To get to our new beginning we are required to get tired of being in the conditions that we're in. Take a stand in growing. Have the focus of getting to that place where God will get the Glory out of our lives.

Don't Look Back

Genesis 19:13-15;17;26
[13]For we will destroy this place, because the cry of them is waxen great before the face of the LORD; and the LORD hath sent us to destroy it.
[14]And Lot went out, and spake unto his sons in law, which married his daughters, and said, Up, get you out of this place; for the LORD will destroy this city. But he seemed as one that mocked unto his sons in law.
[15]And when the morning arose, then the angels hastened Lot, saying, Arise, take thy wife, and thy two daughters, which are here; lest thou be consumed in the iniquity of the city.
[17] And it came to pass, when they had brought them forth abroad, that he said, Escape for thy life; look not behind thee, neither stay thou in all the plain; escape to the mountain, lest thou be consumed.
[26]But his wife looked back from behind him, and she became a pillar of salt.

In the Bible we have heard about the story of Lot who along with his family and servants were delivered from the destruction of the city of Sodom. God gave them favor after hearing their cries. So many were caught up and destroyed in the judgment that was passed down by God. Lot and his family were spared. This is the favor of God that He has for His people. We receive favor and are spared because of our obedient spirit. We experience the same favor today. God delivers us out of the sinful affairs and relationships that are going on in this world. He blesses us with the one that we have prayed about for so long. We find ourselves looking back instead of going forward in the blessings that God has given us, because we do not truly see what we have today.

We must understand that some things that we are in or were in are dead and can never be revived. It would be a wonderful thing if it was possible to revive all situations, but for some relationships, it is not. When we look back, we make it difficult to focus on what we have today. We also have allowed the mess that God has delivered us out of, to come back into our lives. We even drag it into that new relationship that we're in. Looking back is something that God tells us to do.   He tells us this so we can appreciate what we were brought out of. But for some of us, this was not our focus. We take a positive way of doing something that God directs us in and we turn it into a negative thing that He is not pleased with. God tells us this so we do not get caught up reminiscing about what He has brought us out of. We must learn to become focused and aware the way that God wants us to be. When we do, God's blessings will fall on us.

God gave us a commandment. Just as He told Lot, He is telling us today, but we find that we have a disobedient spirit. It sometimes takes over. God does not tell us (all the time), why we have to do what we're suppose to do. We must understand if God tells us, then we must simply do it. God did not tell Lot what the consequences would be if they looked back. In being disobedient, there is always some type of consequence.

Before everything goes completely bad, or gets completely destroyed, God will speak to us and instruct us on what we need to do. God will direct us on how to get to higher ground and how to fix what we're in. Or He will simply deliver us out, but we must learn how to follow. When we're going through, God hears our cries and will move on our behalf to bring us out. Sometimes God speaks to us late in the midnight hour, sometimes in dreams, in the wind that blows through the trees or through other people. No matter how God speaks, we must be ready to hear.

With all the things that God told Lot and his family to do there was one thing that caused the most harm. We must listen to all that God is directing us to do because any one thing that we miss can cause so much harm that it will destroy us forever. We must also understand that what God tells us can be life saving. We must learn to take His word more seriously and move quickly. The one thing that destroyed Lot's wife was being disobedient.

When she looked back she was consumed with the punishment that came down on Sodom and her very life was destroyed. She was delivered out but her disobedience took her back in. Her obedience gave her an escape out of the misery. Her disobedience kept her behind and engulfed her in the judgment. Looking back has greater purpose and greater punishment.

What God is telling us is that we cannot afford to look back when He tells us to go forward. We cannot afford to make the same mistakes that we made before. We cannot afford to go back and lose what we now have gained. We have also seen that looking back could have a negative consequence. It ultimately can kill and destroy everything. If it does not kill us physically, it can kill us mentally. If it does not mentally, then it can spiritually. For some of us, it will destroy in all three areas at once. In going forward we find ourselves getting closer to God. We get closer to all His blessings.

Your Tomorrow

Haggai 2:7-9
[7] And I will shake all nations, and the desire of all nations shall come: and I will fill this house with glory, saith the LORD of hosts.
[8] The silver is mine, and the gold is mine, saith the LORD of hosts.
[9] The glory of this latter house shall be greater than of the former, saith the LORD of hosts: and in this place will I give peace, saith the LORD of hosts.

One of the great things about God is what He does for His people. God takes us through so much, but He has so much more in blessings waiting for us. God wants us to know that He always has more for us. He wants us to look at where we are today and where we were. He goes on to tell us that He is going to give us our desires, just as He did for the nations of old. He will fill the house (home or temple) with Glory. God's desire for us is to give to us and make our lives happy. He wants our lives pleasing not just to Him, but to us, as well. God tells us that He is going to give us more than we had before, but we must be ready and anxiously waiting for our blessings.

We may look at what we had before and say that we have lost so much. When we look at what God has waiting for us, nothing can compare to it. The relationships that we were once in cannot compare to what God is going to give to us in our tomorrow. In leaving the past, in the past we now have the means to open our hearts to the greatness of God. He has infinite blessings waiting for us and we must understand that.

Look at your today and see how things are going. Begin to speak into your tomorrow and begin to believe that God has more coming to you. In going to the next level, God is going to take us higher. He will do this not just for us, but for everyone that will come into contact with us. God wants us to share His goodness with someone else. He wants us to tell someone about that terrible and messed up relationship that we were brought out of and that He can do the same for them. He wants the glory and praise, He so deserves

Trust in God and see that He will do as He has said. God wants the opportunity to bless His people. He wants to give them all that they have wished for, prayed for, and cried for. We must understand that God wants to give to us, but He wants us to become believers. We must have faith that in the morning after the night has gone away, our blessings will come. After the rain falls and the clouds have rolled away, our blessings will come. After we have cried all day and all night, our blessings will come. We must see and believe that God is waiting to give to us. After all that we have been through, we still have the opportunity for more. Grab a hold to that new relationship that God has now placed you in and believe in it. Get a tight grip on that new found friend or love and trust in it. Hold firm to that new home, job and family that you now have and embrace it. In all that you now have, walk in the truth of it. God has given it to you.

Final Thoughts

It is a wonderful thing when we're able to receive the blessings of God. It is a wonderful thing when we look back over our lives and think about the goodness of Jesus. We can now smile because we can see the happiness and peace that we now have. It is amazing that after all that we have been through, God still gives and shows us favor. We can look through all that we have done or allowed in our lives and still are able to walk in the blessings of God.

The reason being, we have done that which we needed to do. We opened our eyes to the truth about where we are and what we're about.   In finding that inner strength that we have lost, due to the pressures of this world, we can begin to take back that which is ours. This is the point when we truly understand the power of God and the power that He has placed inside of us.

We must become believers in our relationships. Believe that if there is any love left for our spouses, then the relationships are not dead. If they are dead, then it does not mean that we're dead. Our lives are not over. God will awaken that spirit inside of us and we will once again believe in ourselves. We will also believe God that our lives will continue. The mindset of defeat is no more. We can begin to live once again and find that new life that is waiting for us.

It is our time. We must leave all that we have lost in the past. We must lay down all that we have, all that we know, and leave the past in the past. Begin the healing process and start to move forward. Today and tomorrow is ours. It is about what we know that makes the difference. We cannot take back our yesterday. We cannot change our present because before we blink it is now our past. The one thing that we do have control over, **is our future**. Don't dwell on the past by looking back at it trying to fix it. Look at it and perfect your tomorrow from its mistakes. It is God's will for us to make it to our tomorrow. We have to use it to make things in our lives better so that we will never want to go back to our past.

Remember, starting over is a blessing, not a curse. When we begin to walk in this knowledge, starting over will not be the worse thing that we have ever done. In doing this, we're now finding ourselves, believing in ourselves, trusting ourselves, and challenging ourselves to be better for the next person that God will bring in to our lives.

> *This is your day, this is your hour, this is your season and this is your life. Leave the past in the past and embrace your new future. For God is going to make all that you have today greater than what you had yesterday.*

Left In The Past

_____
_____
_____
_____
_____
_____
_____
_____
_____
_____
_____
_____
_____
_____
_____
_____
_____
_____
_____
_____
_____
_____
_____
_____
_____
_____
_____
_____

Growing

As

One

When you find that special one that God has
purposed
For you, your life changes.

The two of you change from two separate and
become one.
This change allows life to be all it can be…
(Oh so true!)

Where It All Started

Growing up, even as children, we have wishes, goals, and dreams. One of these dreams is to settle down and be with the one that we will love forever. We yearn to have that endless love that nothing but the love of God is greater. We want a love that nothing here on earth can compare to. We pray that God will give and bring that special one to us. We wait to receive that special one. This is where it all begins. This is also where it will all end. Only in true happiness will all this come true. We must understand the "where's and how's" and apply them to our relationship. We must use everything we have learned from the beginning.

We sometimes feel like none of this will ever come to us because we base it off of what we have had in our lives before; or even what we have in our lives right now. This mindset is not of God. If and when God gives us another chance, we must learn to embrace that chance. We must make it the best we ever had.

We must ask ourselves, what do we really have? What

is it that God has given us? What are we going to do with what He has given us? We now have that chance to change our negative lives' experiences into a positive one. Don't allow a negative mindset to kill your relationship before it has a chance to become something wonderful.

It is the devil's job to keep us from seeing what we have. It is God's job to open our eyes to what we really have. God wants us to see that it is not about the pretty face that makes a healthy relationship grow. It is not in the broadness of his shoulders that makes a lasting relationship. It is two becoming one and growing in oneness. There is a Jewish word that is found in the Torah that deals with just this. The word deals with the thing that has destroyed marriages and it is the thing that can save it, as well. It is all about how it is applied and how important it is in our lives.

It is called BASHERT, a Jewish word, which literally means a match made in heaven, the perfect match or one's predestined soul mate. The one thing that we all must come to grips with is the fact that God has designed a way of life for us. He has prepared and fixed that one person that is intended for us. When your mate comes into your life it will complete the puzzle that you have been trying to finish all your life. There will be no more trying to put together the puzzle with other people that were never equipped with what you really needed or desired. This person can never come to you until you give your life and desires to God. We must allow God to fix it.

Like we said, it is all about where the relationship began

or started that made the difference. We have focused on a man's bank account to size him up. We have looked at how pretty she is to size her up. We have even looked at the size of one's hands, feet and legs to size them up thinking that person is what we needed. All we needed to do was to just stop and look closer and we would have seen that person was not our Bashert. God is giving us another chance, not just to find this person, but also to find ourselves. We need to see who we are and who we are created for, as well.

We tend to place all the blame and requirements on the other person. The same requirements that we have asked God for in that mate, is the same that we must have to offer to our mate. It's a two way street.

We have asked God for so many qualities in that person. How many times have we asked God what type of person do we really need to bring true happiness into our lives? How many times have we asked God what do we need in us to be able to give to our mate? How many times have we asked God to fix us so both of us may give and experience true happiness? How many times have we searched ourselves to see if we have what it takes to show and give to this person? How many times have we asked God if He is pleased with what we're doing? Like it was stated before, it is all about how it starts.

> ### *Revelation 22:13*
> ### *I am Alpha and Omega, the beginning and the end, the first and the last*

God wants us to remember that He is the author of everything that happens in our lives. He knows just what is needed in our lives. He is the Alpha and the Omega; the Beginning and the End. He knows all. We must embrace the fact that God knows who we need and who we don't need. We must embrace the fact that it is all in His knowledge and wisdom of whom we need. We must allow God to bring that person to us and perfect us to what is needed for that person, as well.

So now that we understand that it all started with God, we now know that it will end with Him, just the same. We must search and never stop searching the mysteries of this life. In all of it, find happiness. We must start by starting over and allowing God to make it what it is suppose to be. God wants us to see that if we allow our relationships to start any other way than with Him in the midst, then it is not of Him. Because it is not of Him, it will never last through those bad days that <u>will</u> come and <u>will</u> test ever fiber of that relationship. God never said that we will not have bad days. He never said that it will just work itself out and life will be happy once again. He did say that He will provide for us and will take care of us. It still requires us to make that stand. It begins by making that start today. Live today, search for Him today and find Him today! Allow God to perfect you for that one that He will bring. We are all a work in progress. Just as God is perfecting you for your mate, He is also perfecting your mate for you.

Sacrificing As One

Relationships are looked upon in a strange way. If we're happy then we think our relationships will be happy. When we're sad or upset then we think it will take on that role. This way of thinking is all wrong. We must change the way that we look at the relationships that we're in. We must change our thought patterns to what we expect and to what we want it to be. A relationship is a commitment. It is a dedication of life that we're now in. It is not a country club or a walk in the park. It is a job that requires sacrifice.

What do we really know about this word **"sacrifice"**? We use it all the time. When we want to make a point about someone, we use this word. When we want to express our disposition, we're quick to use this word. Do we really understand the meaning and purpose for this word? Is it just a word that is so common and misused that it really does not mean anything anymore? To understand sacrifice we must first understand the source behind the word. We must look at who did the first true sacrifice and who did the ultimate sacrifice. First, God did the first sacrifice when He gave a piece of Himself to make something else. God did this when He poured out the spirit of life from Himself and put it into man. He did not worry about what He was using or losing. It was about what He was going to gain. Second, God gave His only son to die for this world. He did this to give us a means of getting back that relationship that was once lost with Him.

So we ask ourselves, what does this all mean? What is this sacrifice really all about? It is all about what we or (if we can make it personal) I can do to bring happiness to someone else. It is about thinking about someone else before we think about ourselves. It is about giving and not looking for anything in return. It is about allowing ourselves to be used so that someone else can see the true power of God working through us. It is doing what ever it takes to bring that oneness back. It is about looking outside of the box of normality. It is doing that which is against the normal things of this world. It all lies in sacrificing.

So now we see that we must possess something that this world tells us not to show. We see a lifestyle that goes against everything that we have been taught. If it is applied right, with God in the midst, He will move on our behalf. When we truly allow ourselves to be a blessing to others and truly learn to sacrifice, then happiness comes to us. We will see what living and enjoying life is all about.
Because of the love that we have for our mates, we must learn to sacrifice. The one thing that I have learned is that it is not about what we get that makes us grateful, but about what we're able to give. God has given us the

direction to true happiness. It lies not in <u>what</u>, but it lies in <u>how</u> we give. When true sacrifice is given it comes from the heart. When we give from the heart it is never about what we can get back. It is about God blessing us to be able to help the one we love. It is a wonderful thing to be able to show our love to our mates because we're open, able, and desire to do so.

Keep in mind to truly experience the presence of God we must learn how to sacrifice. We must do it with an unselfish purpose. We must learn to see outside ourselves and become aware of the needs of the person that we're with. When our partner does the same, then the spiritual challenge is on. Now the question is no longer what can we get, but rather, what can we sacrifice and give? We need to ask ourselves how we can show our love even more. How can we be a blessing to them, just as they are a true blessing to us?

When we're willing to sacrifice we do not think about what we're doing; we just do it because it is needed. We do not think about what it will do to us physically, mentally or financially; we just do it. This is just what God wants from us and what the world does not want us to do. We must be mindful of others rather than always being mindful only of ourselves.

There is a negative aspect with always sacrificing. It lies in the fact that there is always someone looking to take advantage of us. They want to use us until they cannot use us anymore. This is a major problem. It can tax a person to their very core. We sometimes find the person we're with do not have the same mindset of sacrifice; neither

then ask ourselves, what are we doing and are we really
suppose to be doing these things? We know relationships
are not a one way street. We know it should not only
favor one person. God recognizes this and He is telling
us that it is not right. It is not for us to give and give
and give and sacrifice and get nothing in return. This
situation is one in which we must apply wisdom. We
must have wisdom in what we do and we must have
knowledge in what we show.

It is not a give and get nothing type of world. It is a world
where we sacrifice together. We grow in the struggles of
giving together and we find happiness in what we're able
to do together. This is why we cannot do this for just
anyone. This type of sacrifice is reserved for that one that
understands sacrifice, as we do. This is for that one that
is willing to look outside of them selves and sacrifice for
us, just as we will for them. This is for that person that
is purposed to you. What's important is the growth that
comes out of a person and into the other person.

We must stop sacrificing just to be sacrificing, but begin
to do it with the purpose that God has ordained. When
we're able to do this, then we will truly be blessed and
honored for our sacrifices.

Receiving As One

There are benefits in all that we do and all that we say. There are rewards for the good deeds that we are blessed to do for others, besides just showing that we care. We have struggled and we have sacrificed so much for the ones that we love. Sometimes we sacrifice for those who we do not even know. God has seen all of this and now has reserved this time for us to be blessed. It's our time to receive for all that we have given.

For some people, it is not a problem in receiving from others. We can even receive from a perfect stranger. Why can we not receive from that person that God has placed in our lives? Why can we give all but can never receive, even a little from that person? Why can we go out of our way for them but when it is our turn, there is a major problem. How can we allow ourselves to get to this stage? How can we be so neglectful to the feelings that they have about giving to us? Why do we hinder their blessings?

These questions have confused so many. Some of the best

relationships have ended and no one could understand why. The answer is not how this happened, but why it happened? How did we allow a good person that wanted to help us slip through our fingers? Why did we allow this person to leave and make someone else happy? How did we miss the fact that what they wanted to do for us was just as important as what we have done for them? The reasons lie in our past.

We have allowed our past to infect us with a poison of selfishness. It sounds funny, but it is so true. We want to receive. We complain about not receiving. The truth is some of us don't know how to receive. We always want to be the person that gives. It makes us happy. When we look back we can not see that we really were being selfish. We're selfish because we always give and never allow anyone to give to us. We're in control. What about that other person's joy in giving? Why do we take that away from them?

We think it is all about what we're able to give to a person that defines the love and caring that we have for them. We must understand it is also about the receiving that defines that relationship, as well. As we have stated before, there are so many things that we must look at; and receiving is one of them.

> *Genesis 26:2-3;6-10;12*
> *[2] And the LORD appeared unto him, and said, Go not down into Egypt; dwell in the land which I shall tell thee of:*
> *[3] Sojourn in this land, and I will be with thee, and will bless thee; for unto thee, and unto thy seed, I will give all*

> *these countries, and I will perform the oath which I sware unto Abraham thy father;*
> *[6] And Isaac dwelt in Gerar:*
> *[7] And the men of the place asked him of his wife; and he said, She is my sister: for he feared to say, She is my wife; lest, said he, the men of the place should kill me for Rebekah; because she was fair to look upon.*
> *[8] And it came to pass, when he had been there a long time, that Abimelech king of the Philistines looked out at a window, and saw, and, behold, Isaac was sporting with Rebekah his wife.*
> *[9] And Abimelech called Isaac, and said, Behold, of a surety she is thy wife: and how saidst thou, She is my sister? And Isaac said unto him, Because I said, Lest I die for her.*
> *[10] And Abimelech said, What is this thou hast done unto us? one of the people might lightly have lien with thy wife, and thou shouldest have brought guiltiness upon us.*
> *[12] Then Isaac sowed in that land, and received in the same year an hundredfold: and the LORD blessed him.*

In order to understand the receiving part of being one, we must first understand that it is all about what God has waiting for us. It is about giving our all and making the person who we're with more important than anything else. We must be willing to do whatever it takes to keep happiness in our relationship. Isaac had two missions. He was to be obedient to the voice of God. He also was to keep the one that he was with happy. We miss this in our relationships and then we try to fix it by either trying to buy or lie our way back into good grace with them both.

God is showing that if we treasure who we have, then we will see the sacrifices that are needed. More importantly, we will receive what is ours from them. In all that Isaac did, God gave not just to him favor, but He gave it to both, him and his wife. Receiving as one is the true blessing in receiving. When we can receive and it is appreciated, as well as loved, by the both of us, it will bring us closer than we were before.

We must understand and master the art of receiving in an unselfish manner. We must learn to receive not just from other people, family members, and even from ourselves, but learn to receive from the one that love us. We must allow the act of receiving to give both of us pleasure and happiness. God is looking and waiting to give because we're both acting as one. Also, because of whom we're willing to give to and receive from.

We shouldn't close our minds to the blessings that God want to give us. Today is our day. It is our year and season to receive. We must receive our blessings and allow God to show us how to love that one. We must allow ourselves to see how much they appreciate, care and love us.

Bringing It All Together

Why is it an issue when it comes to being one? Why do we struggle when we deal with or talk about making decisions with the one that we're with? We have seen marriages, families, and other relationships become divided over simple issues that deal with decision making. We have talked about it with everyone. We cannot seem to find a solution to this problem. What is the problem? Why can we not find happiness in being one? Why have we become divided in so many areas of oneness? Why is it so hard to give and receive? Why can we not look beyond how the world views the way we make decisions?

Divisions, as well as, so many other issues run through our homes and through our families. Some of us have gotten tired of asking why, but we must not give up. We cannot afford to throw in the towel and give in. We have exhausted all of our resources trying to find that which was missing. Some people never find out until it is too late and the relationship is over. We must stop looking at our surroundings and our up bringing. We must look to God for our directions and our answers. With failure, we have tried to manage our lives through the world's system. We have tried to live according to how psychologist have stated and have failed. We have even tried numerous chat and counsel sessions and they have failed also.

We have gone through several relationships and have tried to do what is right in them, but they never last. We must ask ourselves why? We need to ask ourselves, what are we doing wrong? We should ask, what needs to be changed and what direction is a real relationship suppose to go. We have not seen and listened enough to God. God is telling us how to get to the point where oneness is the foundation of our relationships.

> **St. Matthew 19:5-6**
> **[5] And said, For this cause shall a man leave father and mother, and shall cleave to his wife: and they twain shall be one flesh?**
> **[6] Wherefore they are no more twain, but one flesh. What therefore God hath joined together, let not man put asunder.**

Now that we understand, the question is not what is going wrong, but what is missing? Sometimes oneness has left the relationship. Sometimes oneness was never there to begin with. We have gotten into relationships and even into marriages, but never established oneness. God says that we were once twain or two, but now are one. We have to learn and understand what this means. God does not look at the two people that are married as two, but looks at them as one. Just as we're walking with God, we must be one with Him. We must also be one in our relationships. God's desire is to bring oneness into a relationship. The devil's desire is to bring division. God is looking to bring happiness to the one (both husband and wife) not to the two (individuals). We must learn to understand this. God says for us to leave where we are and join with the one that we are with, and become one.

St. Matthew
[5] And said, For this cause shall a man leave father and mother, and shall cleave to his wife: and they twain shall be one flesh?

We miss so much when we have the wrong spirit working in our relationships. We experience too many issues when we close our minds to the fact that we're one and not two. We must look outside the physical and focus on the spiritual aspects, as well as the true growth of our relationship. We must become more focused on the other person rather than on ourselves. We must become more concerned with being on one accord and working together. What are we saying? We must look past ourselves and within our partners. Look to fulfill their desires. We must look at the other person to see ourselves. We need to see how much more there is and can be. In doing this, we will begin to work at things the way that God has always designed for it to be. This opens the window for true blessings to be poured out into our lives.

Final Thoughts

We know that God has so much waiting for us. We know that He has blessing upon blessing just sitting in His Holy bag waiting for us. We must allow Him to open it and pour it out unto us that we would not have room enough to receive. We have to understand that we do not deserve any of it. We do not deserve any of the blessings that God desires to give to us, but because God is a merciful God, we can now receive what He has for us.

A lot of times we fail to understand that God is looking to bless us as one in our relationships. We fail to understand that we're viewed as one. When we commit to each other, we commit as one to God. The blessings that are waiting for us are blessings directed to us for being as one.

We must take this oneness to another level and see the full benefits of it. We must understand that it is work. It requires every positive thing that we can find in it to make it work. We must always keep God first in it and in everything.

If we want our relationships to work, we must look at

how God is with us and understand that our relationships with each other are just the same. We must learn that receiving is just as important as giving and this is even true with God. God is the author of the giving factor. He wants us to embrace this same way of giving and receiving. Just imagine what will happen if we were to give more. Most of all, God wants us to understand we're one in our relationships just as we're one with Him.

Look at what we've committed to and see what level of sacrifice we need for ourselves, as well as how much sacrifice is needed from our mates. It is an equal amount of giving and taking that is required, but in all, it is all about the growing that is to take place.

We can't allow our past to stop us from being who we are. We can't allow our past to stop the one that we love from being them selves. The person that God has given us is there for a reason and a purpose. God gave them to us for they were predestined for us from the beginning. We must look for our Bashert. We must look for that one that will fit our puzzle of life and will grow with us all the days of our life.

It is not what we can give and receive by ourselves, but it is about what we can give and receive as one. This will make the difference in how happy, how much in love we are and how much we will share together.

Growing As One Notes

_____

_____

_____

_____

_____

_____

_____

_____

_____

_____

_____

_____

_____

_____

_____

_____

_____

_____

_____

_____

_____

_____

_____

_____

_____

_____

_____

_____

_____

_____

_____

_____

Tribute

To begin, I must first thank God for all of His mercy and grace. I want to give Him all the glory for the wisdom, the knowledge and the understanding that he has given me. It was God that put these words into my head and it was God that directed my fingers in writing this book.

I would like to thank God for two special women that I cherish; first; my wife (Mrs. Michelle Pearson), the love of my life. She was the inspiration behind this book. Only God knows where I would be, if He had not blessed her to be by my side. She brought balance and showed me that there was another level of love.

Second, my mother (Mrs. Catherine Pearson) is the one that showed me, through her life, that you never give up. There are always options. She taught me that if you keep God first, then there is no struggle, no pain, no sacrifice and no setback that could ever keep a Child of God down.

This book is dedicated to my wife and kids (Ronald,

Devin, Delisha, Deonna) who are my everything.

My mother taught me long ago that it is all about the family. I thank God for all my brothers and sisters (Terri, Valerie, Elese, Marlene, Geneine, Kimberly, Mario, Ivan and Cornelius).

Special Thanks

Because of their sacrifice, this book was made possible. In believing in this ministry they became financial supporters.

- My wife Michelle Pearson and my kids
- Marlene Willis and family
- Ivan Pearson and family
- Mrs. Catherine Pearson (mother)
- Cornelius Pearson and family
- Joshua Zapf
- Dove Data Corporation
- Mario Pearson and family
- Sean Reveals and family
- Pastor D.C. Perkins (Perfect Praise Church)
- Reginald Dukes and family

God Bless You All For Your Support

About The Author

Minister Octavius Pearson began preaching the gospel over 10 years ago in the city of Detroit. He began at Gospel Tabernacle Apostolic Church under the pastoral of Elder Michael T. Martin. Several years later he relocated to Indianapolis, IN and continued working. Soon after his relocation he was inspired to reach the world through internet ministry and spiritual writings. Minister Octavius spoke to and directed many all over the country with his words.

He then began a march that has led him in a passionate direction. His desire is to reach the world with thoughtful truths and wisdom ministry where people can become more inquisitive to God and His word.

Minister Octavius Pearson
Email: living_truth@email.com
Livingtruth.vze.com

CPSIA information can be obtained
at www.ICGtesting.com
Printed in the USA
FFOW02n1506100216
21333FF

9 781425 997113